TALK ABOUT A MURDER

A Comedy Mystery Play

LEE MUELLER

Copyright © 1996 by Lee Mueller

All rights reserved.

No part of this book may be reproduced in any form or by any electronic or mechanical means, including information storage and retrieval systems, without written permission from the author, except for the use of brief quotations in a book review.

Caution: Professionals and amateurs are hereby advised that TALK ABOUT A MURDER! is subject to a royalty. It is fully protected under the copyright laws of the United States of America and of all countries covered by International

FOREWORD

Thank you for taking the time to read this play. I would like you, the reader, to know I do not mean this to be a great theatrical work of art. I am aware of classic works written for the stage, and I have been an actor in several; I have also been an actor in murder mystery dinner theatre productions. Two different worlds. This murder mystery comedy was composed with a particular audience in mind. An audience who were fans of this genre of theatre - light entertainment, simple plot, simple mystery, and hopefully, lots of laughs. As a playwright, I attempted to pull this genre up from some cartoonish style scripts that were out there -stuffed with double entendres and grade school humor, but not overhauling it too much. Just lifting it up slightly. Again, this is not Serious Theatrical Literature, but hopefully still entertaining.

-Lee Mueller

INTRODUCTION

"Talk About A Murder" was originally titled *"Some Show"*, essentially because at the time of writing it, I couldn't come up with a good title and referred to it as; *"some show about a murder"*. "Some Show" as a title stuck with me and I also imagined that many people going to see the play really didn't know the name and would tell friends, "Oh we're going to see... some show." It wasn't until a handful of years later that I realized fans of murder mystery theatre loved plays with "murder" or "death" in the title – hence the name change. At the time of writing the play, it seemed everyone in the entertainment industry had their very own talk show. I took that idea and ran with it.

ACT I

Ideally, the set will be a makeshift "location" studio for a television broadcast. Wherever this play is performed it should be as if -accommodations were made for the show. Since it is "On The Road with Nickie and Ricky Rivers" and they are broadcasting from any given location - it should be minimal setting for their talk show with "talk show" style chairs or a couch sit center. Phoebe's demonstration counter is back off to the side.

Preshow: Stagehand and perhaps camera Person do busywork (perhaps the Announcer too). Closer to start time, Ricky and Nickie enter and mingle with the crowd. Maybe coach the crowd and practice big applause before the start of the show.

House lights down. Them music starts.

ANNOUNCER: (*set up offstage out of sight, perhaps in the back*) Ladies and gentlemen, coming to you direct from a local access cable channel near you, it's the Ricky and Nickie Rivers Show! Tonight's episode comes to you live from (your town) as part of their "On the Road with Ricky and Nickie" tour. Tonight's special guests include Shecky Scagnetti and Edie Buffet, domestic diva Phoebe St. Self, gossip columnist Polly Pettegolo and more. So without further delay and with much adieu, please put your hands together for ... Ricky and Nickie Riverrrrrrrrrssss!

Music fades during applause. Ricky and Nickie run onto the stage excitedly. A super-sugary amateur version of Regis & Kelly. They alternate speaking to the live audience, to each other, and to the camera.

RICKY: Hello everyone!

NICKIE: Good evening. What a great crowd!

RICKY: Well, Nickie! Here we are!

NICKIE: Yes. We are! We are here! It's great to be HERE ... with all these lovely people!

RICKY: Yes, it's great to be here in ... uh ...

NICKIE: In *(your town)*.

RICKY: Right! Exactly! It's great to be here.

RICKY and NICKIE briefly ad-lib about people in the crowd.

NICKIE: What a wonderful time we've been having on the road with our "On the Road with Ricky and Nickie" tour. Haven't we, Ricky?

RICKY: Right you are, Nickie! Going across this great big land of ours and seeing all the ... great big land and the ... great big people.

Both laugh superficially.

ACT I

NICKIE: Stop it, you politically incorrect man! Seriously, you all look fabulous. What an adventure it has been. Especially in that last city we were in.

RICKY: Right you are Nickie! There was some kind of crazy mix up, the audience thought there was going to be a tractor pull or monster truck show. Well, needless to say, the crowd was less than happy to see us.

NICKIE: A tad hostile. They began pelting us with cheese fries and corn dogs!

RICKY: And you know, that Cheese Whiz will just not wash out of a good cotton-polyester blend.

NICKIE: And it can be the dickens to get out of your hair.

Both laugh.

RICKY: And just so everyone here is clear, there will be no tractor pull tonight!

NICKIE: There may be some *leg*-pulling, but no tractors!

Both let out obviously fake laughter.

NICKIE & RICKY: (*inhale, then simultaneously*) Anyway ...

RICKY: We really do have some show for you tonight.

NICKIE: I can hardly wait! What kind of show is it? Is it one of our confrontational shows? You know, where we reunite someone with a jilted lover or crazed stalker?

RICKY: No Nickie.

NICKIE: How about child stars who are now serving

hard time?

RICKY: Negative Nickie.

NICKIE: Secret crushes? I love secret crush shows!

RICKY: Sorry, honey.

NICKIE: Please tell me it's not a diet show or one of those self-empowerment deals.

RICKY: Nickie, we have gathered a group of very talented people. People just like us!

NICKIE: Oh. A recovery show?

RICKY: No, sweetie. I mean, people like us who are talented, and who will soon have their very own TV shows!

NICKIE: (*not excited*) Really? A plug show? The producers couldn't come up with anything?

RICKY: Actually Doctor Dunn canceled at the last minute.

NICKIE: Doctor who?

RICKY: Doctor Dunn, author of "Positive Thinking To A Thinner You." He couldn't make it.

NICKIE: Really? What was he thinking?

RICKY But anyway folks, we could stand here and talk about people who have canceled on *us* all night.

NICKIE: Really! Left us high and dry. Just because we don't pull in the big numbers. Low market share. People who think they're better than...

RICKY: You know Nickie, we have to go to a commercial right now, and ...

NICKIE: And just because we've jumped networks a few times and ended up on cable, I mean really!

RICKY: And I mean we have to go to a commercial!

NICKIE: Whatever! Stay tuned. We'll be right back!

As announcer starts the dialogue, stagehand comes out to Ricky and Nickie with note cards, straightens Ricky's tie, Nickie's hair, etc.

ANNOUNCER: The Ricky and Nickie Rivers show — live from (*your Town*) — is brought to you by Sweet Prince Sleep Aids. For those restless nights when you don't know whether to be or not to be tired, Sweet Prince will help you get to sleep, perchance to dream. Available in pill or gel cap form. When you need a good night, Sweet Prince is the answer. (*beat, then quickly*) Possible side effects include headaches, vomiting and constipation. If relaxation lasts longer than four hours, consult a physician. (*normal speed*) Now once again ... heeeere's Ricky and Nickie Riveeerrrs!

RICKY: Welcome back. Our first guests are a husband and wife singing sensation.

NICKIE: At one time they headlined the biggest lounges in Vegas, Tahoe and Schenectady.

RICKY: And soon, they will have their very own show on a local access cable channel in your area. Please put your hands together for ...

NICKIE: The lovely and talented ...

RICKY: Shecky Scagnetti and Edie Buffet!

Music up. Shecky and Edie enter. They greet each other with hugs and handshakes. Music fades.

NICKIE: Welcome to the show! You both look fabulous!

EDIE: Thank you. You guys look fabulous too! Don't they, Shecky? They look much taller in person.

SHECKY: Right you are there, Edie. And let me just say, it is a delight and a sincere sensation for us to be here on your show. And I mean that.

EDIE: And such a swell town and a great place. Ain't it, Sheck?

SHECKY: Yes it is, pumpkin. Of all the (*your location e.g. theatre, school, banquet halls etc.*) we've ever performed in, this one is by far the most ... recent. (*beat*) Say, Edie, didn't we do this room for a Kiwanis Christmas party in '06.

EDIE: No, dear. That was a VFW Hall in (*a nearby town*).

SHECKY: Oh right. Seems like we spent a week there one night. (*Makes his own drum rim shot sound.*) I wanna tell ya.

NICKIE: You two are so funny!

EDIE: And we just love your show. You two are so wonderful together.

RICKY: Thank you. Speaking of which, you guys will have your own show soon, won't you?

EDIE: That's right, Ricky. Me and Shecky will be having our own show soon.

ACT I

Pause as Ricky anticipates more.

RICKY: Well, tell us about it.

EDIE: Oh. Well, me and Shecky were just gettin' tired of travelin' and singin', singin' and travelin'.

SHECKY: From Natchez to Mobile ...

EDIE: From Memphis to St Joe ...

SHECKY: Wherever the four winds blow ...

EDIE: We've been in some big towns ...

NICKIE: And I bet you heard some big talk.

EDIE: Did we ever! So anywho, we was doin' some show in Cleveland, and our agent calls us!

SHECKY: He says, "Kids, how would you like your own show? There's a big market for this *reality* stuff! And I said really? Reality? Who knew? I didn't!

EDIE: Cuz Shecky and me were never fans of reality.

NICKIE: I can imagine.

EDIE: So, he says they want to send this camera crew to follow us around. Ya know, watch us do whatever we do.

SHECKY: I says to the guy, I says, as long as they don't follow me into the toilet, you got yourself a deal! And then Bada bing, bada boom. We got our own show.

NICKIE: What a fascinating story.

EDIE: Oh it is! And our show will have a lot of fascinatin' reality things. Won't it, Sheck?

SHECKY: It's gonna be like a reality show and a talk show all in one, but different.

RICKY: Well, that's different.

SHECKY: Sure it is! Reality show wrapped up in a variety show format!

EDIE: And a cookin' show.

NICKIE: Ok Wait, it's what now?

SHECKY: A real variety of talking and cooking. But with a country slant. Edie and me are getting into country music. It's the new thing these days!

RICKY: You two don't strike me as country music people. Are you?

SHECKY: Well, you gotta follow the money Rick! If the money's good enough, we'll learn to love it. Right, sweet lumps?

EDIE: Oh yeah. Me and Shecky have been learnin' how to sing through our noses!

SHECKY: And I tell you what, it does wonders for the sinuses!

NICKIE: Let me see if I follow you. It's a "reality, talk cooking show"? And you are going to be singing country songs?

SHECKY: Sure! But hey, we aren't ditchin' the standards! We have Vegas in our blood. We'll mix in some Sinatra along with the hillbilly crap.

ACT I

EDIE: It ain't Hillbilly crap honey, it's very beautiful music.

SHECKY: Whatever. Hey, if it makes money, I'll sing about pick up trucks and six-packs.

EDIE: And, of course, we'll have all the BIG country stars hanging around, being all real and junk.

NICKIE: It sounds absolutely enchanting.

RICKY: Do you have a name for your show yet?

SHECKY: Yeah, it's called "Real Down Home with Slim Scagnetti and Bubba Buffet." Airing this fall, Mondays at 3 am, on local access channel 173.

NICKIE: Well, we'll be sure to watch it. Won't we, Ricky?

RICKY: We sure will. Thanks for joining us today, guys. (*turns*) Now, our next guest is ...

SHECKY: Hey! Our *next* what? Wait a minute here! That's it?

RICKY: What do you mean, Shecky?

SHECKY: I mean, that's it? That's all the time we get? We don't get to sing or nothin'?

RICKY: Maybe later, if time allows. We have to keep the show moving along. You know how it is. Only so much time for each segment.

SHECKY: Segment-schmegment. You two took all that time flapping your traps about tractor racing corn dogs and you only asked us like two questions!

NICKIE: Just be a love, Shecky, and let us do our show. When you do your reality cooking country show, you can flap your trap all you want.

SHECKY: You got that right, toots. I'm gunna do some trap flappin!

RICKY: And.. our next guest is well-known to housewives across America.

NICKIE: She is the Queen of Crafts and the Baroness of Better Housekeeping.

RICKY: And she too, will soon have her own show on the Divine Home Domestic network. Please welcome ...

NICKIE: The lovely and talented ...

RICKY: Phoebe St. Self!

Music up. Phoebe enters and sits. Music fades.

RICKY: Welcome to the show Phoebe.

PHOBE: It's a pleasure to be here, Richard.

RICKY: Please. Call me Ricky.

PHOEBE: If you wish. But I must warn you about my formality. I just feel that it is respectful to address people by their proper names.

RICKY: Well, you don't need to feel proper around us, Phoebe.

PHOEBE: Please, I prefer *Mrs. St. Self*. And I am well aware of your lack of formality, which is why I feel it is my duty to introduce proper etiquette to this program.

ACT I

NICKIE: (*sardonic*) Why, thank you. I was going to pick up some etiquette this morning, but they were sold out.

RICKY: Uh.. thank you Mrs. St. Self. For.. introducing proper.. things to our show.

PHOEBE: You're welcome, I'm sure.

RICKY: So, Mrs. St. Self, we understand you will soon have your own show, tell us about it.

PHOEBE: You are correct. It is entitled "At Home with St. Self" and it ...

EDIE: Hey! That's kinda like Shecky and me's show. Isn't it, Shecky?

SHECKY: That's right, Edie. "Real Down Home With Scagnetti and Buffet." This fall on channel 173.

PHOEBE: (*clears throat*) As I was saying, my show will focus on "domestic engineering."

NICKIE: Domestic engineering? You mean, housework?

PHOEBE: Yes, you may call it that, if you wish.

NICKIE: I wish. Ricky and I can't afford subtitles, so forgive me if I translate.

RICKY: Nickie, please! You were saying Mrs. St. Self?

PHOEBE: Yes, I was about to say that I feel women have lost touch with their place within the home environment. Their sense of duty and obligation has withered. They spend too much time on their careers and not enough time pursuing important matters, such as home aesthetics. Women these days are too busy being doctors, lawyers, senators, and even ... talk show hosts. They have forgotten traditional values. For instance, I was appalled to learn that most women do not know the proper clockwise motion required to efficiently clean a pane of glass.

NICKIE: No!*(sarcastic)*Really? Well, I say, stop the madness! What an outrage!

RICKY: Well, Phoebe ... I mean, Mrs. St. Self ... I understand you're going to show us how to make a creative home decoration today. Let's head over to the counter and get our hands dirty.

PHOEBE: *(as they walk)* Well, no one will be getting dirty. At least not me. But I will show you how to make a sinfully luxurious paper chain streamer.

NICKIE: This should be TV gold! *(at the counter)* So, speaking of chains, you said that women shouldn't have careers?

PHOEBE: I believe their careers should be their homes and families. They should be able to prepare lovely meals for their husbands and children. Too many women are relying on "drive-thru nutrition" instead of experiencing the wonders of a food processor or crockpot.

NICKIE: Well, you've got the "crock" part of it right.

Phoebe shoots Nickie a look.

RICKY: *(trying to steer things back)* So we're going to make luxurious paper chains.

PHOEBE: That's correct. This is a simple creation anyone can do at home using scissors, glue and recycled magazines. Of course, I use discarded copies of House Beautiful. First, we take our scissors and cut strips of no more than one-inch wide. Like so.

All three start cutting strips as they talk.

NICKIE: And like so.. on this new show, you're going to talk about, what? Vacuuming? Dusting? How to make a tea cozy out of crepe paper?

PHOEBE: Funny. As a matter of fact, we will discuss the best way to vacuum certain types of carpets. For instance, did you know that double-stitched Wool blends are best cleaned at a 45-degree angle?

EDIE: Really? Is that how you get them little sweeper lines all goin' the same way?

PHOEBE: Actually, it's because the fabric is sewn at a defined angle and it's best to approach it with suction at alternate angles against the weave for maximum cleaning effect.

EDIE: Oh! Is that a fact? What did she say Shecky?

SHECKY: I have no idea.

RICKY: Any advice for getting Cheese Whiz out of a cotton shirt?

PHOEBE: You might try a little club soda and vinegar. You might also try simply wearing an apron. It will protect your garments from stray food particles.

NICKIE: An apron?

PHOEBE: Yes, an *apron*. It's a wonderful invention. Every housewife has one. Perhaps if you ever find the occasion to step into a kitchen, someone will point one out to you.

NICKIE: *(threatening with a forced smile)* You do realize I have a pair of scissors in my hands.

RICKY: Ladies, please! Well, I seem to be having a bit of trouble getting my paper strips even.

PHOEBE: Here, Richard, let me show you a nifty trick. First, fold the sheet over twice. Then cut evenly on both sides. Like so. And wah-lah. Four evenly sized strips.

NICKIE: *(using voice to mimic Phoebe)* Four evenly sized strips. Neener neener neener!

PHOEBE: I beg your pardon?

RICKY: So, Mrs. St Self.. when can we expect to see your new show?

PHOEBE: My program will begin airing this fall in the early afternoon. This is when I feel most real women will have time to enjoy my show.

NICKIE: Phoebe, maybe you should consider putting your show on late at night with all those other useful domestic engineering programs, like the handy dandy food chopper and the Super Dooper Smoothie machine!

PHOEBE: I do not appreciate your sarcastic tone, Mrs. Rivers.

NICKIE: I don't think you appreciate much of anything, do you?

ACT I

PHOEBE: *(getting more intense)* I appreciate many things. A place for everything and everything in its place. I appreciate the look of a neat and orderly house. And I *love* the smell of Pine-Sol in the morning. *(inhales, eyes closed)* It smells like victory.

RICKY: So ... we know how to cut the paper strips. Let's move ahead to the final creation.

PHOEBE: Certainly. After cutting the strips, you loop them and gently glue them together into a lovely chain. And what you end up with is ...

Phoebe holds up an elaborate (pre-set) completed chain. Ricky encourages the audience to applaud. Nickie half-heartedly goes along.

EDIE: Can I ask Mrs. Saint a question? I always wondered: Is it all right to vacuum a Velvet Elvis paintin'?

PHOEBE: Um ... I'm not sure.

NICKIE: You're not sure?! Well, Phoebe, perhaps if you spent more time at home and less time marching around vacuuming up women's rights and teaching people nonsense they learned in first grade...

PHOEBE: Excuse me! I did not come here tonight to be ridiculed! I don't need to stand here and take your snide remarks.

NICKIE: Then don't. I'm sure there's a yellow waxy build-up somewhere out there that requires the proper clockwise motion.

RICKY: Please! As I stated at the beginning Nickie, this is *not* one of our *confrontational* shows.

NICKIE: I'm sorry, Ricky.

RICKY: Let's head back to the seats.

They return to chairs.

NICKIE: Sorry, folks. I just lost my head for a moment. *(suddenly perky again)* Is it back on? OK! I'm fine now. Please continue, sweetheart.

RICKY: OK. Our next guest has been called the Princess of the New Age of Enlightenment. She's an astrologer, a psychic, a druid, *and* ... a certified public accountant.

NICKIE: And, she has a new talk show debuting this fall on the Chakra Cable Network. Please welcome ...

RICKY: The lovely and talented ...

NICKIE: Celeste Ethereal!

Music up. Celeste enters and sits. Music fades.

RICKY: Welcome to the show, Celeste!

NICKIE: Or is it Ms. Ethereal? *(smarmy glance at Phoebe)*

CELESTE: No, Celeste is cool. I must say, it's a very moving experience for me to be here this evening. To feel the energy in this room. The positive vibrations. The love.

RICKY: So, you can actually feel "energy" in the room? And vibrations?

CELESTE: Oh yes. Many vibrations.

SHECKY: Hey, I was feeling "vibrations" too, but I thought it was a truck rollin' by or the burrito I had for lunch.

EDIE: You're such a stinker Shecky!

SHECKY: Ya don't have to tell me!

NICKIE: So tell us about your show, Celeste.

CELESTE: Yea for sure, well, it will be a physic talk show.

RICKY: A Physic talk show?

SHECKY: What, you sit around and read each other's minds?

EDIE: I knew you were going to say that!

SHECKY: I guess if you know what they're gonna say, there's no sense in asking any questions. *(To audience)* Am I right or what?

CELESTE: *(To Shecky)* You're an amusing man with a delightfully small aura. *(To Nickie)* No, what I plan to do is like.. "channel" spirits from the nether plane to speak through me. But like, you know, in the talk show type of trip. What I plan to do is interview celebrity guests from the great beyond.

RICKY: Really? Dead celebrities? Wow! Who might we expect to see ... or hear on your show?

CELESTE: Well, I have connections with Jerry Garcia, Janis Joplin, as well as Bertholt Brecht and Soupy Sales.

RICKY: What a diverse group there Celeste! Could you ring one of them up now?

CELESTE: Now? You mean, right now? Well, I don't know if the conditions are right.

SHECKY: What do you need, babe? Some incense? A lava lamp? I think Edie may have a mood ring if that helps.

CELESTE: No, I need time to connect to the spirit plane. Sometimes it takes hours just to get a good connection. I can't just snap my fingers and "ring" someone up. It takes a great deal of meditation.

PHOEBE: Meditation? You mean medi*ca*tion! You New Age weirdos are just a bunch of hopped-up hippies.

RICKY: Now that was uncalled for, Mrs. St. Self.

CELESTE: Yes. You don't need to be a negative vibe merchant. The spirit guides around you don't like it.

PHOEBE: Well, I don't like it either. I don't like any of this. This hocus-pocus is just a bunch of mumbo-jumbo.

EDIE: No, it ain't! Shecky and me visited Physic one night, and they told us we'd be "makin' a major decision soon." And it all came true.

RICKY: And what was this "major decision"?

EDIE: Either it was where we decided on cutting the Kurt Kobain retrospective from our act.. or when we decided to cut dairy from our diet.

SHECKY: Cuttin' the dairy was tough, let me tell ya. I can't milk the jokes like I used too. But I'll give it a shot. This guy walks into a doctor's office and says, "Doc, I got this terrible problem. I can't remember anything for more

ACT I

than a second." Doctor says, "How long have ya had this problem?" The guy says, "What problem?"

Celeste closes eyes and lets forth a moan.

SHECKY: *(playing off moan)* What, you didn't like that one? How 'bout this: A guy walks into a bar holding a platypus ...

PHOEBE: *(stands)* Pardon me, but I wish to leave. This is a show I no longer wish to be part of.

NICKIE: My goodness, Mrs. St. Self, you just ended your sentence in a preposition. Come now, have we no decency?

PHOEBE: I most certainly did no such thing.

RICKY: No, Nickie's right. You said "no longer wish to be part OF."

EDIE: Yeah. I heard it. She did say "Part OF." I heard that part.

PHOEBE: As if you would know proper grammar, you dizzy lounge heathen!

EDIE: *(stands)* Who you callin' dizzy?

CELESTE: Oh no. The hostility vapors are causing a physic blockage in my retina. *(Holds her eye.)*

PHOEBE: I thought this was a halfway respectable show. But "halfway" is giving you people too much credit. And that's just what you people are — too much! This is nothing more than a circus sideshow!

NICKIE: If the respectability factor is too low for you, you are more than welcome to take your Saintly Self and respectfully remove it from the stage! Or as we low-life, working women say, "Don't let the door hit you where the Good Lord split you!"

RICKY: Nickie!

NICKIE: *(pointing to Phoebe)* If this is what staying at home and making nifty keen dinners for your family, does for you, then I'm glad I'm here tonight!

PHOEBE: Well, I'm not! This whole show is a joke!

SHECKY: Joke? A grasshopper walks into a bar. Bartender says, "Hey! You know we got a drink named after you." The grasshopper says, "Really? You gotta drink named Murray?"

PHOEBE: You see! You have no control! No decorum. This isn't a talk show! It's more like ... a barroom brawl!

The following dialogue between Phoebe and Ricky should be simultaneous. In each other's faces.

NICKIE: I've had enough of your holier than thou attitude! You and your macrame making craft weasels are just a bunch of frustrated cronies who can't get real jobs, or a purpose in life, so you dream up a fantasy world where housework is some kind of specialized career that requires a Ph.D. from M.I.T. Well, let me tell you something, Phoebe St. Full of Herself ...

PHOEBE: *(starting on Nickie's 'Thou')* Me? Holier than thou? What about you prancing around the stage like you're in a high school musical? When my husband comes home at night, I can be proud of the perfect atmosphere I've created with my own two hands. I'm not off pretending I'm some big smarty-pants TV star, while dust and filth litter my coffee table ...

As this confrontation begins, the stagehand runs out and tries to break it up. Celeste falls into a trance and begins some sort of chant. Edie and Shecky stand up and encourage the brawl. Ricky does not interact. Phoebe storms off and the announcer's voice drowns out the stage noise, restoring order.

ANNOUNCER: Do you feel stressed? Are you feeling rushed? Tense? Like the whole world is crashing down upon you? Do you feel you're in need of a good B-complex vitamin supplement? Well, relax. Take it easy. Take some of that stress and worry away. Try Johnson and Masters Brand Mineral Oil. Full of the rich B-complex vitamins your system needs to feel at peace. It also contains a heaping helping of helpful iron and minerals that attack stress and tension where it starts. Johnson and Masters Mineral Oil will have you feeling cool, calm and collected. Ask for it by name. Also, try it in the "new and improved" two-liter size. So, chill out with Johnson and Masters Mineral Oil. In regular, cherry and kiwi flavors. And now, once again ... heeeeere's Ricky and Nickie!

NICKIE: Welcome back. Our guests tonight are ... Shecky Scagnetti and Edie Buffet.

RICKY: And Celeste Ethereal, who was just about to channel someone up for us. Go ahead, Celeste.

NICKIE: Yeah, Celeste. The "negative vibe merchant" is gone.

CELESTE: *(eyes closed - moans)* Calling all occupants of interstellar planetary realms. I am connecting to the vortex and reversing the polarity of the neutron flow. I am channel surfing the sphere of the spiritual continuum. *(she pounds her fist two times)* Who's there?

SHECKY: Orange! Orange who? Orange you glad I didn't say banana!

EDIE: Be quiet Shecky! She's channel surfing somebody!

CELESTE: Who wishes to speak through me? Yes. Oh? Huh-uh. Oh no ... *(she moans and drops her head)*

EDIE: Is she all right?

SHECKY: Maybe they're calling collect.

CELESTE: *(springs to life, but still in trance)* Wait. My spirit guide Ariel is trying to tell me something. She has a message for someone in the audience here tonight. *(She stands and walks into the first row of people.)* Does someone here tonight have a first name that begins with the letter S. If so, please raise your hand. (Hopefully, a number of people raise their hands. Celeste picks one.) You. Is your name... Shar...Sann... Salll...Sarah? *(Response: "Susie" or whoever.)* That's right, it's (repeats correct name). I have a message for you Sarah.

SHECKY: Hey, if you run into by late Uncle Morty in there, I have a message for him. He still owes me money!

CELESTE: What's that, Ariel? Sandy did what? Really? No kidding? Susie, is there a person in your life named Bob? *(If no, offer Bill, Tom, John, etc., until you get a yes.)* Does (Bob) drive a car? Does it have four wheels? *(Yes response.)* I knew that. What is Bob's relationship to you? *(ad lib for a minute, then end with something like ...)* Sharon, Ariel wants me to tell you something about (Bob) that will have a huge impact on your future. The most important thing you need to know about Bob ... is ... Hello? Ariel? Oh no ... *(snapping out of trance)* I'm sorry, I'm losing the connection.

SHECKY: Can you hear me now?

EDIE: Shecky!

CELESTE: It's gone. My chakras are clogged.

SHECKY: Try jiggling the handle.

CELESTE: There's too much bad energy residue in this area. If I could just go off for a little while and cleanse my aura and align my pathways.

SHECKY: Sure babe, the can is down the hall and to the left.

RICKY: Of course. By all means.

Celeste exits.

NICKIE: Well, Ricky.

RICKY: Yes, Nickie?

NICKIE: It's been some show so far, hasn't it?

RICKY: It sure has, and now I believe it's time to bring out our final guest.

NICKIE: *(to herself -sarcastic)* Oh great there's more. *(sighs and then overly cheerful)* Right you are, Ricky! Our final guest tonight is no stranger to this show.

RICKY: She was a correspondent for TMZ, renowned Television critic and restaurant reviewer for the Salvation Army bulletin.

NICKIE: And now she's the host of her own talk show called "Celebrities Get Real"! Here she is ...

RICKY: The lovely and talented ...

NICKIE: Polly Pettegolo!

Music up. Polly enters. Music fades.

RICKY: Welcome again, Polly!

POLLY: Thank you, darlings. Say, this has really turned into quite the little show tonight. I thought it was going to be one of those boring plug shows. You know, everyone coming out here saying, "Watch my show, watch my show!" But it has gotten really interesting.

NICKIE: Well, it is ratings week, after all.

RICKY: That's right. Hopefully, you'll give us a good review.

POLLY: I said the show has been *interesting*, that doesn't imply *good*. Maybe if you had a human sacrifice, then it would be something.

SHECKY: Speaking of something, there's something familiar about you, don't I know you from somewhere?

POLLY: Probably. Everyone knows me and I know everyone. I should say I know *things* about everyone. Everyone who's *anyone* that is.

RICKY: So, are you familiar with any of our other guests tonight?

POLLY: Yes, I am ashamed to admit it, but I saw Edie and Shecky many years ago at some show in Chicago. It was a retrospective of Jay Z tunes done with the Cicero Chamber Orchestra. You know, even if Shecky and Edie had a sense of rhythm, it still would have been awful.

EDIE: Don't be a hater Polly!

RICKY: Tell us about your new talk show, Polly.

POLLY: Well, it's called "Celebrities Get Real." It's essentially a survival-style show. Celebrities will be lured into awkward situations and be forced to fend for themselves.

NICKIE: Fascinating! So what type of situations will you have?

POLLY: Well, on one episode, Kevin Costner and Keanu Reeves will have to act their way out of a giant paper bag. In another episode, Beyonce will have to sing live.

NICKIE: That's cruel. What else?

POLLY: Well, if they survive the ordeal, they will have the opportunity to stop anyone negative press I may have dug up. I will have a giant rake they can halt. Of course, as in muckraking.

SHECKY: Can we say "muck" on the air?

POLLY: Speaking of which, I should have been out here earlier. I happened to rake up some dirt on that St. Self woman. Did you know back in '95 she used to go by the name Lola St. Self? That prissy, cold-hearted prude used to be a Vegas showgirl.

NICKIE: Phoebe St. Self was a Vegas showgirl?

POLLY: Yes! I'm surprised Shecky didn't know her. He knew all the showgirls at one time.

SHECKY: Huh? It wasn't at *one time*! It was over a span of years! But seriously, I don't remember her. I remember 99 broads but Phoebe ain't one.

EDIE: I thought she looked a little familiar.

Celeste screams and runs out.

CELESTE: Danger! Bad vibes! Creepy Karma!

[Stagehand grabs her and pulls her back.]

POLLY: What one Earth was that?

RICKY: I'm not quite sure.

SHECKY: I'm not sure it was of this Earth!

RICKY: So, Polly, your show is called "Celebrities Get Real," right?

POLLY: Uh .. Yes, that's right. This fall on Real TV.

NICKIE: Well, it sounds absolutely charming, and I'm sure we'll watch it.

RICKY: So long as you don't feature us on it.

POLLY: Well, I thought about having Nickie in an episode where they pull her in a red flyer around a Hotel bar. Just to see how long she can stay on the wagon.

[Celeste enters.]

NICKIE: Wait, what? Did you say wagon? What does she mean about ...

RICKY: Oh, look, everyone! Celeste is back! Welcome back, Celeste!

CELESTE: I'm sorry about my little traumatic episode a minute ago. That usually doesn't happen to me. Someone from the spirit plane was trying to get in touch with me and warn me about something.

RICKY: Trying to get in touch with you?

CELESTE: Yes. I was mentally reaching into the astral thither to bring it hither, when all of a sudden, I heard someone calling me.

SHECKY: You oughta just get an answering machine, babe.

CELESTE: Someone was trying to tell me ... Danger ... Hate ... Evil ... Muuurrrder!

POLLY: Danger?

RICKY: Hate?

EDIE: Evil?

NICKIE: Muuurrrder?

POLLY: Well, that would certainly help the ratings.

CELESTE: But it's gone. I got out my crystals, wrapped myself in white light, chanted my favorite Yoko Ono song, and it went away. They stopped trying to call.

SHECKY: Probably a wrong number.

NICKIE: It was probably the Yoko Ono song.

[There is a scream offstage.]

RICKY: No, *that* was the Yoko Ono song.

EDIE: I think it came from backstage.

STAGEHAND: (*running on, out of breath*) I uh ... just wanted to ... I had to tell you ... that ... I think you need to know ... She's ... gone ... horrible!

SHECKY: Easy for him to say.

STAGEHAND: Feeb ... Feeb ...

RICKY: Feeb? Phoebe?

POLLY: Who's Feeb Phoebe?

SHECKY: I knew a Feeb Franklin once. Had a dancing poodle act in the Catskills.

STAGEHAND: No ... Phoebe ... is dead!

RICKY: Phoebe is dead? Mrs. St. Self? How?

NICKIE: Here, dear. Have a seat!

[forces other guests down.]

STAGEHAND: (*sits*) I don't know. Just dead. It was horrible.

NICKIE: (*back in talk show mode*) Really. So, this death, tell us a little about it.

STAGEHAND: Well, she was yelling that she couldn't find something and wanted somebody to call her a cab, and then she started in about the crackers we had because they were stale. You know, I told them we needed to get fresh crackers, but somebody thought we could just serve the cheese fries and corndogs we had leftover from last night. So, no one went and got any fresh stuff to serve tonight, and the crackers were stale ...

RICKY: (*interrupting*) Die?! How did she die?!

STAGEHAND: Oh yeah, that. Umm, I don't know. She just died. I mean, nobody was in there with her, not like anyone wanted to even get near her, so I went to tell her about the cab she wanted me to call, and the crackers, and ... she was dead.

RICKY: Dead. Just dead?

STAGEHAND: Yes. Just lying there on the floor ... all dead and ... not moving, like someone who's ... you know, dead. With this sparkly stuff all over.

NICKIE: Sparkly stuff? Interesting. Tell us about that.

STAGEHAND: Well, I didn't get too close but it kinda looked like those crystal things that Celeste had.

CELESTE: My crystals! Oh no. Now they have "dead vibes" all over them.

[Candy Kafka enters reluctantly. She wears a book-bag and carries a folder and textbooks.]

CANDY: Umm ... Hi. Sorry to interrupt the show..

RICKY: Who's she?

STAGEHAND: Oh, that's Candy. She's Phoebe's bodyguard.

CANDY: Actually, I'm just sort of filling in, as it were. My brother Bubba is actually her bodyguard, but he couldn't make it tonight, so I'm here and ... Oh man, I guess I didn't do a very good job. My brother is going to be considerably upset. I was supposed to look after Mrs. St. Self while she was in town. I had to cut class tonight. I just went out for a moment and ... this is not good.

RICKY: I'm still trying to get past the "she just died" part.

CANDY: Well, it appears that way, but you see, the reason she needed protection ... I mean, it may have been some sort of delusional paranoia, which one could attribute to her pseudo-celebrity status and all ...

RICKY: I'm sorry, her what?

CANDY: What I mean is, she was convinced that someone was out to "get" her. So while she may have "passed on" in a "natural" manner, it's a little curious and, may I speculate, the means would lend themselves to be considered "un"-natural.

SHECKY: I understood that about halfway through that. Like the first five words.

CANDY: I am not a police person or anything, but I did take some classes in criminal investigation for my degree in Art History. And since it was my job to protect Mrs. St. Self, I am required to ask you all to remain in this building until the proper authorities can procure a full investigation.

POLLY: Are you implying one of us may have killed Phoebe?

CANDY: Yes, you could call it an implication.

POLLY: Hey, that's great! One of us is a murderer! Oh, this is good!

RICKY: But, excuse me, this is not good! We're doing a show here.

NICKIE: Fascinating! Yes, you're right, Polly! This is good! Very good! Suspense. Mystery. Intrigue. (*To audience*) All right, new show, everyone!

RICKY: No. No, it's not.

[Buzz enters.]

BUZZ: All right. What's all this then?

RICKY: Who is this now?

BUZZ: Buzz Becket, bunko squad. We just happened to be staking out an illegal Bingo game in the area. Whereupon I observed screaming and pursued the sounds to this location. Upon entering, I observed the body of a female lying prostrate upon the floor.

SHECKY: What was on the floor?

NICKIE: We think she was murdered!

BUZZ: Murder, huh? Well, homicide isn't my area of expertise, but ...

RICKY: Wait! Hold on! We're doing a show here!

BUZZ: A show? (*looks around*)

RICKY: This is a talk show! We're live!

SHECKY: Phoebe's not.

BUZZ: Talk show? (*To Nickie*) I'll need to ask some questions of you and Regis.

RICKY: Ricky! Ricky Rivers. This is the Ricky and Nickie Rivers show! We're broadcasting this very moment and now everything is ruined! Let's just cut!

NICKIE: No! There's no cutting! We're not cutting! We're going to keep going!

RICKY: Keep going?

NICKIE: Don't you see? This is great, Ricky! This is way better than any Springer or Povich show! We've got a real-life murder right here on our show!

CANDY: Guys? OK. I didn't say she was "murdered." I merely implied that the circumstances would lead me to believe that could be a possibility.

SHECKY: Is it me? Or does anyone hear a bunch of words coming out of her mouth, but they're all jumbled?

BUZZ: (*to Candy*) And you are?

EDIE: She's the bodyguard.

BUZZ: Bodyguard? Whose bodyguard?

RICKY: The late Mrs. St. Self.

CANDY: Well, not a "real" bodyguard. I did take a tai-chi class, though.

BUZZ: What's all this business about "circumstances" and "murder."

CANDY: Oh, that. Well, Mrs. St. Self had an uneasy feeling about being on this show tonight. (*she begins digging through backpack*) She sent my brother this documentation with background checks on all the guests. I assume she was under the impression that she was in danger. (*still digging*) Maybe one of the guests here tonight could cause her some type of harm.

CELESTE: I got that same vibe.

BUZZ: Vibe, huh? And you are?

CANDY: That's Celeste Ethereal. Psychic and CPA. (*Finally pulls out papers*) Here it is. Mrs. St. Self didn't indicate much about Celeste. I guess she didn't know too much about her.

CELESTE: But she may have known me in a previous life.

BUZZ: Let me see this. (*Takes papers from Candy*) "Contract of Protection for Fo-bee St. Self."

NICKIE: No, it's Phoebe. Phoebe St. Self.

BUZZ: Uh-huh. (*reads*) "In the event of fatality, please be advised: one or more such persons acting as said guests of talk show named The Ricky and Nickie Rivers Show, on or about (*the actual date*) may have cause to inflict fatality to myself, signed Fo-bee ...

NICKIE: Phoebe!

BUZZ: ... *Phoebe* St. Self.

CANDY: But as you see, it doesn't specify "who" she was afraid of. She virtually had something on everyone.

BUZZ: (*reading*) Sheldon Scagnetti and Edie Buffet.

SHECKY & EDIE: Huh?

CANDY: Apparently, Mrs. St. Self was acquainted with the aforementioned party many years ago. They both were employed in Las Vegas. Back then, Mrs. St. Self's name was Lola. And this Lola was an exotic dancer and a showgirl.

RICKY: So you're saying ... Her name was Lola? She was a showgirl?

POLLY: Sorry, folks, but I already broke that story.

SHECKY: I never knew any Lola in Vegas.

EDIE: Sure you did, Sheck. The Pit Boss at the

Sahara had a little poodle named Lola.

SHECKY: I thought he had a Great Dane named Hamlet.

BUZZ: (*reads*) Polly Petty-gallow.

POLLY: That's Pettegolo. Petta-go-lo.

CANDY: Pettegolo. That's Italian for gossip. Just a bit of trivia I learned when I was in Italy for my... anyway, I believe Polly's name is on the list because she and Mrs. St. Self had a running feud for years. You see, Polly writes a gossip column and wrote some horrid things about Phoebe in the paper.

POLLY: It's a dirty job but someone had to do it.

CANDY: In fact, here's a clipping from the Weekly World that was particularly interesting.

BUZZ: (*reads*) Fo-bee St. Self ...

Nickie clears her throat.

BUZZ: *Phoebe* St. Self made a dreadful spectacle of herself last night on the Home Shopping Channel. Pawning off her Cozy Making Kit for 49.95 was the most desperately pathetic attempt at marketing this reporter has ever seen. Someone should make a cozy for this woman's head and relieve us of her presence.

POLLY: Oh, well ... that. Yes, you see ... I was referring to her presence on television. Not her life.

RICKY: This is all well and good, and I'm glad we're ...

BUZZ: (*to Candy*) I see you have quite a catalog of the populous present this evening. Tell me, which of the potential suspects was in the area of the victim at the time of the perpetration?

SHECKY: Now what the heck is he sayin'?

NICKIE: That's what's so intriguing, officer. No one was. At the time Phoebe was backstage, all of us were out here.

BUZZ: So, in other words, she vacated this location and all of you were assembled in this region?

NICKIE: Uh ... no, we were in here.

BUZZ: That's what I said, ma'am.

NICKIE: It was?

BUZZ: Yes. All of you were here, correct?

POLLY: Hold on one moment. All of us were here, except for Celeste. She was off ... in some other world.

CELESTE: Sorry, I am incapable of harm. It's a bad karma thing to do.

BUZZ: So, except for Celeste, no one else was in proximity to the deceased?

NICKIE: Well, the stagehand, of course. And Her. (*points to Candy*)

CANDY: OK. See, while this is true, I was in her proximity, it's not entirely true the entire time.

RICKY: What do you mean?

BUZZ: (*to Ricky*) I'll handle this. (*to Candy*) What do you mean?

CANDY: Well, what I mean is, I had to leave her proximity for a period of time.

RICKY: Why did you leave? You're the bodyguard.

BUZZ: Sir! (*beat*) So, why did you leave? You're the bodyguard.

CANDY: Well, Mrs. St. Self has an acute obsession with germs. In a slightly compulsive manner. She has to have anti-bacterial pre-moistened towelettes. Unfortunately, I brought the wrong kind, the non-anti-bacterial type. So, I left to see if I could find some and when I came back, she was ... well, you know.

STAGEHAND: (*excited*) Oh! Oh! That's the other thing! She had one in her hand!

BUZZ: One in her hand?

STAGEHAND: Yeah. A little towelette thing. Clutched in her hand!

CANDY: I don't see how that's possible. She didn't have any.

NICKIE: Fascinating!

RICKY: Yes, this is all great stuff, but we need to take a commercial break here. We are doing a show and ...

BUZZ: Fine, fine. That will give me time to fully secure the backstage area and question all the individuals with connections to the location of the transgression.

SHECKY: What language is that?

EDIE: It's cop-speak.

SHECKY: Oh! 10-4!

CANDY: Oh, one more thing. You might want to question him too. (*pointing up*)

BUZZ: Him? (*looks up*)

CANDY: Yes. Him.

RICKY: Him who? (*looking up*)

CANDY: You know. Him. (*pointing up*)

NICKIE: God?

CANDY: No, the announcer!

NICKIE: Oh! You mean, Don Godot.

BUZZ: Don Godot? Where is he?

NICKIE: He never comes near the stage.

BUZZ: I'll wait for him.

RICKY: Great. While you wait for Godot, can we please take a commercial break?

BUZZ: All right, you may. I want to study these reports and the crime scene further. But don't go anywhere!

NICKIE: (*to audience*) That's right! Don't go anywhere! Because we'll be right back with our fascinating murder mystery show, right after these important messages!

ANNOUNCER: The Ricky and Nickie Rivers show will return right after ... (*insert your own dialogue here if serving dessert or going to intermission*)

ACT II

ANNOUNCER: Ladies and gentlemen, welcome back to the second half of the Ricky and Nickie Rivers show!

[Theme music starts. Nickie and Ricky enter with guests.]

ANNOUNCER: (*cont.*) Just look at this studio, filled with fabulous suspects! So, please welcome our very special guest hosts, and your investigators for the evening, Buuhhhz Beckett and Candy KaaaahhhhfKaaah!

[Buzz and Candy enter.]

CANDY: (*awkwardly*) Um ... Hi. Welcome to the ... investigation.

BUZZ: Affirmative you are there, Candace. Tonight, we have a very special investigation for you.

CANDY: Yes, Buzz, we do.

RICKY: OK. Cut! This is a stupid idea! This is getting way out of hand! We were having a fairly decent show here in ... um ...

NICKIE: *(your town)*!

RICKY: In (town) and everything was going along fine, and then one of the guests has a.. heart attack or some fatal ailment backstage, and suddenly everyone's going off the rails on a crazy train! Talking about foul play and murder and suspects! And now, you people just wander out here, right in the middle of our show, with your so-called "investigation." What do you have to go on? Huh? Nothing! There's no evidence of any foul play! She wasn't shot. She wasn't stabbed. She wasn't anything. The only thing she was, was mad. She got mad and walked off the show. Just walked off and died. No big deal. It happens all the time.

BUZZ: What happens all the time?

RICKY: Stuff! Stuff happens! All the time. People die all the time. There doesn't have to be a reason.

CANDY: I had a philosophy class where we discussed that very issue. "And when you gaze into an abyss, the abyss also gazes into you." Anyway, I must digress. (*pulls out a plastic baggy with towelette inside*) The issue regarding tonight's events should be one of cause and effect. The effect was Mrs. St. Self's death and this ... (*shakes bag*) was the cause.

STAGEHAND: That's the thing she had in her hand. Remember, when I was saying that she had a thing in her hand. A towelette thing? Well, that thing *(pointing to baggy)* is the thing!

CANDY: And she used it right before she died.

SHECKY: So? My uncle Bernie died with a Weed Whacker in his hand. Just keeled over when he was outside whacking the weeds. Couldn't pry the thing loose. Had to bury him with it.

RICKY: OK. So the towelette is the last thing she used. She wiped her hands with it. So?

CANDY: Well, as you recall, she didn't have one. She wanted an "anti-bacterial" version, I only had the plain moist kind. This! This is an anti-bacterial" wipe! Where did this one come from?

RICKY: Maybe she found one after you left.

BUZZ: Maybe someone gave her one.

NICKIE: Gave her the kind she needed and then what? She anti-bacterial-ized herself to death with it? Seriously! How could that kill her?

CANDY: Because someone tainted it with the extract of the Ubangi River Newt.

POLLY: The Ubangi who?

CANDY: The Ubangi River Newt. A lizard indigenous to the Congo region.

RICKY: You have got to be kidding me!

EDIE: No actually she's not! I saw somethin' on the Discovery Channel about that! I watch TV late at night after our gigs to unwind. I love the animal show. Especially the spider monkeys. Anyway, I remember the newt program. They have like poison spit or somethin'.

CANDY: Correct you are Ms. Buffet. The expectorant of the River Newt is highly toxic. In fact, deadly. Even a small amount placed upon the epidermis can be fatal.

SHECKY: What did she just say?

POLLY: I think she said if the Newt spits, don't wear it.

RICKY: Let me get this straight. Someone had this ... river lizard newt ... and they had it spit on a towelette and then gave it to Phoebe? *(to Candy)* Are you crazy? You know how far fetched that sounds? Are you a poison river newt expert or something?

CANDY: Well, actually I had a class in Zoology at (*local community college*), and I wrote a paper on exotic secretions. I recall that the fluid emitted from the Ubangi River Newt has the distinct aroma of stale mangos.

[Candy *opens bag and sniffs. Holds it out for others to smell. They all move away.*]

CANDY: No, really, it's all right. The odor is harmless. You just can't get it on your skin. If you do it paralyzes your respiratory system and you die instantly.

CELESTE: Yes! Yes! The towelette! I'm picking up strong psychic waves ... or maybe they're particles, not sure. They're either waves or particles ... or maybe some fuzzy combination of both ...

SHECKY: Somebody shoot me.

CELESTE: It's evil! Bad evil! Bad evil poison towelette bag!

BUZZ: Thank you, Miss Ethereal, but we've already ascertained that information.

POLLY: But the information we don't have is where did she get it? (*to Candy*) You said she didn't have a towelette. And none of us could have given it to her. We were all out here.

BUZZ: That is, all except for Miss Ethereal. You were offstage for a brief interval, am I correct?

NICKIE: Yes. She was clearing her channels or something new agey like that.

CELESTE: Mr. officer Buzz, I swear to ... whatever deity or deities you may follow, I didn't do anything while I was gone. I mean, yeah, there are times when I'm meditating and I drift far out there and I'm not totally aware of what my body's doing while I'm gone. But I wouldn't harm anyone. I mean, if my corporal body did something bad such as ... oh, kill someone while my mind was on another plane ... I'm sure it would tell me when I got back. Leave a message or something.

STAGEHAND: OK. I can pretty much vouch for Celeste. I was back there, you know, offstage, back there ... and I saw her. I mean, Celeste. I saw Celeste. I saw her pretty much the whole time. She was sitting in the corner doing her yoga or whatever meditation thing. Just "om-ing" and stuff. She didn't move the whole time. Well, there was that thing where she started freaking out and was running around yelling "Danger" and stuff. I was chasing her around trying to catch her so, as I said, I can vouch that her "body," as it were, didn't kill nobody.

BUZZ: Is that right?

RICKY: So, there you have it. No one was near Phoebe at all.

CANDY: But I think we're missing an important fact here.

SHECKY: I think I'm missing a lot here. I got lost right after the spitting frog thing.

EDIE: A spittin' newt, Shecky! Weren't you listenin'? Somebody put poison on Phoebe's little thing, and when she wiped her hands, it killed her. And then, we were all tryin' to figure out who could've done it. But see, we were all out here on the show. Except for Celeste, who's body was back there, but her mind wasn't.

SHECKY: (*rolling eyes*) Thanks, Edie. I'm up to speed now.

CANDY: Let me bring you all up to speed with a question that I would like to pose. Yes, you were all out here during the show, but where were you *before* the show?

NICKIE: Right! Right before the show! One of us could have done it then!

SHECKY: Done what then?

NICKIE: Yes, done what then?

ACT II

CANDY: Well, gotten to Phoebe's purse. (*digs in backpack*)

NICKIE: Her purse?

SHECKY: OK. I'm lost again. What purse?

CANDY: (*pulls out purse*) This purse.

SHECKY: Whose purse? What's with this purse thing?

BUZZ: Mrs. St. Self's purse was located near her self in an open fashion.

CANDY: When she was looking for a towelette, I asked her if she checked her purse and she said she didn't have to. She knew for a fact that she didn't have one in it.

BUZZ: And then, upon proceeding into the room after her demise, her left hand was clutching a used towelette, allegedly saturated with said poison. Whereupon I observed at this time, her purse to be the source from whence the towelette originated from.

POLLY: Wait, what?

EDIE: Somethin' about her purse.

SHECKY: Again with the purse!

CANDY: Yes. It appears for intents and purposes, it would appear Mrs. St. Self checked her purse anyway. Possibly, an unconscious uncertainty forced her to look into the purse.

CELESTE: Yes! The purse! I'm getting something, something about the purse.

SHECKY: Well, I'm not. I'm done with the purse.

CELESTE: Ariel has another message for me ... a message about Phoebe. Yes, Ariel, show me. Oh ... I can see it ... and feel Phoebe's thoughts. She's unsure about wiping her hands. Maybe ... maybe in the purse! No! Yes! Maybe. What's that, Ariel? OK. She opens ... opens the purse to see ... see ... see the evil towelette. Bad towelette! Hands. Hands being wiped. Wiping. Sting! Hot! Oooh, hot evil bad skin feeling. Danger! Can't breathe! Darkness. Fading.

EDIE: So anyway... someone put the towelette in her purse when she wasn't lookin'.

SHECKY: You got all that from this?

NICKIE: Of course! One of us could have planted it there before the show.

RICKY: How do you know someone planted it there?

CANDY: Well, (*digs into purse*) because of this! (*holds up towelette packet*)

RICKY: And that is ...?

CANDY: Insurance.

SHECKY: All right, I'm lost again. And I sure ain't talking about insurance.

CANDY: What I mean is, *this* is insurance that Mrs. St. Self would receive a fatal amount. This is another packet that remains sealed.

RICKY: So she got in from her purse but why would she look in there if she was sure she didn't have one?

BUZZ: Who knows?

SHECKY: Who cares?

CANDY: Perhaps she was looking for something else and just happened to find them. At least one of them. (*holding up packet*)

BUZZ: You better let me have that, Ms. Kafka. (*takes packet from her*) I'll have it dusted for prints and tested at the lab.

RICKY: Do you want to tell me how on earth someone would get this poison, this so-called Newt saliva into one of those towelettes?

BUZZ: It could have been manufactured by the perpetrator to appear as the genuine article. Or one could use a common household syringe to inject the hazardous liquid into the package.

POLLY: What I don't get is, why go to all the trouble? I mean, if someone wanted to kill Phoebe, there are a lot of easier methods.

BUZZ: And what might those methods be, Ms. Pettegolo?

POLLY: Well, what I mean is ... injecting some kind of rare poison into a sealed towelette. There's intercontinental travel involved. Jungles. Newts. Towelettes. It's all so sordid. And why tonight? Why this show?

BUZZ: Maybe their intention was for her to die on stage.

NICKIE: Now that would have been great!

SHECKY: Nah! I've died on stage lots of times. It's no big deal.

BUZZ: You do raise a valid point. It does seem peculiar that this incident occurred on this particular evening, during this particular presentation. And that the methodology of murder was so meticulous.

CANDY: Yes. The killer had to know Phoebe would

be here tonight. And they would have to know a lot about her. Such as her habits. The compulsive hand wiping. And that she only used those pre-packaged, pre-moistened anti-bacterial towelettes.

NICKIE: That raises the question of how many of you knew who the other guests would be?

EDIE: Me and Shecky didn't know till we got here, did we, Sheck?

SHECKY: I'm still not sure I know who's here tonight.

CANDY: Did anyone know in advance that Mrs. St. Self would be here?

POLLY: Well, I knew who the other guests would be, but I always do. It's my business. It gives me time to, you know, dig up the dirt, as it were. You never know when you may need a little venom to ... well, no, I don't mean venom as in "venom" — like the poison type. I mean, as in gossip. You know, juicy stuff. Well, not "juicy" as in anything toxic or like a secreted type of poison. What I mean is ...

RICKY: Polly! Polly! We understand.

CELESTE: Well, I knew who the other guests would be too. But like..no one told me. I saw it in a vision, many months ago. I was sitting in a vortex in Sedona, Arizona.

BUZZ: So some of you knew in advance that Phoebe St. Self would be present this evening?

[They all respond accordingly.]

BUZZ: (*cont*) And you, Miss Kafka, were her contracted guardian for this evening, correct?

CANDY: Well, no, my brother was. I'm just filling in.

BUZZ: And you're filling in because ... ?

CANDY: Because he had tickets for (*whatever event may be occurring nearby ... hockey game, etc.*)

BUZZ: And did you know any time before this evening that this particular event would require your attention?

CANDY: Actually, I just found out a few hours ago.

BUZZ: So, which one of you came onto the program first this evening?

EDIE: That would be Shecky and me.

BUZZ: So, Mr. Scagnetti and Ms. Buffet were out here the whole time during which Mrs. St Self was present. That would mean Miss Ethereal and Ms. Pettegolo would have been backstage for a period of time in the general region of Mrs. St. Self's property, that being her purse. This fact would have given either one of them a window of opportunity to deposit the tainted towelettes.

POLLY: Excuse me, but I don't kill people with poison. I use the pen!

CANDY: Interesting. (*thinking*) Hmmm ...

[They all look at Candy.]

POLLY: You want to share with the group, darling?

CANDY: Something Polly just said reminded me of something I recall from my criminal investigation classes. There is this concept called "motive." It usually proves to be very important. Now, if Polly had been killed this evening, the motive would have been pretty easy to assume.

POLLY: I beg your pardon?

CANDY: No offense, but you do write some pretty unkind things about people. Someone may seek revenge by ... making sure you never write another negative thing. But why Phoebe? I mean, she could be annoying and tyrannical, but that doesn't warrant murder.

SHECKY: It doesn't?

BUZZ: No, there must be something deeply rooted here. Something from the past. A long-standing grudge, or ...

STAGEHAND: Or maybe it was this crazed fan-stalker-killer guy who was obsessed with her, and he had like a million pictures of her in his room, you know, plastered all over his walls. And he had written all these weird letters to her, and she never answered and so he flipped! You know, just like snapped. So he gets this big red magic marker and drew these big X's through her pictures and ripped them all down and tore them into a million pieces and took them out into his backyard and burned them up and buried the ashes in a shallow grave. And then he tracks her down here tonight and gave her a towelette!

[All look at the stagehand for a few beats.]

STAGEHAND: Or not. I'm just saying.

BUZZ: So ... Mr. Scagnetti, according to the investigative background search, you and Mrs. St. Self were employed at the same Nevada hotel.

SHECKY: I told you before, I didn't know any dame named Lola. I knew a Lana, a Lulu, a Lannie, a Lori, and a Lecresha ... but no Lola!

BUZZ: Did you have any sense of familiarity with the female decedent who was present earlier this evening?

SHECKY: *(looks around)* Anyone care to translate here?

NICKIE: I think he wants to know if you've ever met the snotty little woman who is no longer alive.

SHECKY: Oh. No. Not really.

EDIE: She *did* look familiar to me.

BUZZ: She did?

EDIE: I might have seen her picture in Good Housekeepin' or somethin' when I was at the dentist's office. Maybe that's where I know her from.

SHECKY: I never saw her before tonight. And like I said, we didn't know who was going to be here tonight.

BUZZ: (*to Nickie and Ricky*) Which one of you invited her onto the show?

NICKIE: That would have to be my dear husband, Ricky. I couldn't stand the women. Of course, I don't mean I couldn't stand her enough to "kill" her or anything. Just the usual animosity. You know.

RICKY: Well, I invited her only because she fit with our theme. She was starting her own TV show. That's why *all* these people are here tonight.

BUZZ: So, only a few of you knew she would be here, and only a few of you were backstage at the designated time. Since there were no witnesses, and whatever evidence we have is circumstantial, I cannot say we have much of a case. I'm afraid I will have to forgo any further investigation. We have reached a proverbial stalemate.

CANDY: Stalemate? You think so? What about the crystals on the body and the fact that Celeste was offstage. Yes, it's circumstantial but it's something, right?

SHECKY: Yea it's something all right. I'm not sure what but something happened.

CANDY: There's something happening here. What it is, ain't exactly clear. (*beat*) Phoebe knew someone was out to get her, and they got her. They accomplished it without anyone seeing or hearing or knowing anything about it.

BUZZ: There's no clear motive. No substantial opportunity. I say we terminate the investigation and notify the proper contingent of law enforcement authorities.

CANDY: (*sighs*) I guess he's right. We don't have much to go on. No clear motives. No witnesses. Besides, I have a paper due tomorrow on The Metamorphosis and I ...

STAGEHAND: You're all giving up too easy! I see all kinds of junk here! Look at Shecky! It's obvious he's lying about not knowing Phoebe! He probably had a wild affair with her and dumped her because he was afraid Edie would find out. So Phoebe, who was actually Lola then, started blackmailing Shecky to get money. Money to start her own show!

POLLY: Oh, that's good. I like that. (*Takes out pen and pad. Writes it down*)

STAGEHAND: And Polly with the whole gossip thing. Maybe Phoebe had dug up some juicy dirt on Polly to get back at her and she found out before the show and killed her to keep her quiet!

[*All look at stagehand. He looks around and waits a few beats with embarrassment.*]

STAGEHAND: Just a thought. I think I've been working on talk shows too long.

NICKIE: Wait! That's it! Talk show! (*crossing into audience*)

RICKY: What? What are you doing?

NICKIE: When you're not prepared or can't think of what to do, you turn it over to the audience! Let them do the work for you! That's what I'm doing, Ricky!

RICKY: I see.

NICKIE: I know that some of you are just dying to ask some of these people here on our show ... or should I say, "suspects" and you're dying to ask them some questions. Does anyone have any questions for anyone here?

[At this point the audience may or may not need a little prompting to get questions rolling. Nickie may ad-lib to help this along. The best way found to control the questions because experience has shown that once the audience catches on that the actors are 'open season' - the questions multiply, is to wrap up by stating, "two more questions, one more question." This usually returns the control back to the actors. Upon control being returned ...]

RICKY: Alright. Let's see what we have here ... (*ad lib a summation of what was revealed during the audience Q&A*) What do you think, Nickie?

NICKIE: It's anyone's guess, Ricky. What do you think, Mr. Buzz?

BUZZ: I think that we should turn this over to the appropriate authorities.

NICKIE: I think we should turn it over to the audience!

STAGEHAND: Oh yeah! Like those murder mystery dinner things where they let the audience vote.

RICKY: What a stupid idea! Let *them* decide? Aren't these the same people who pelted us with cheese fries?

NICKIE: No, honey, that was in (*a nearby town*) I think it's a fabulous idea! In fact, these lovely people here tonight already have (*little pencils and paper or insert your own voting method*) They can vote for the suspect they think did it. Was it Shecky or Edie? Polly? Celeste? Me?

RICKY: Nickie, please!

NICKIE: Oh, sorry, hon. Or Ricky! We can have the crew collect the votes. Come on, this will be fun times!

[At this point, the cast collects votes as they are completed by the audience. Of course, remaining in character and interacting with the audience. Once the votes have been collected and to regain control of the production ...]

NICKIE: OK, everyone, it's time to continue the show. This is fascinating! Everyone is a suspect! It's just like playing Clue or something!

VOICE: (*offstage*) It was Colonel Ketchup in the drawing-room with a monkey wrench!

SHECKY: Oh great! Now we're getting heckled!

NICKIE: (*looking to audience*) We've never been heckled! This is great!

VOICE: (*offstage*) Mrs. Mustard in the basement with a broomstick!

RICKY: OK. Very funny to the point of becoming annoying.

NICKIE: Who's doing that?

[They all move to look out at audience. As they do, Sissy enters and takes a seat. Sissy is the same actress who was Phoebe, only she is very toughly dressed — perhaps a leather jacket, black fishnets, boots — somewhere between a biker chick and an exotic dancer.]

SISSY: It was Tony Montana in the shower with a chainsaw.

[They all turn around and see Sissy.]

RICKY: She's alive!

CELESTE: She's returned to us from the other side! This is so beautiful ... yet trippy!

EDIE: How did she ...? How did you ...?

POLLY: What's up with the outfit? Is that the Street Corner Collection from Walmart?

CANDY: Mrs. St. Self! Are you OK?

SISSY: Me? Yep. I am Okie dokie, smokey. But it sure doesn't look my sister's fared too well.

CANDY: Sister? Phoebe was your sister?

SISSY: Don't worry yourself none. It happens all the time.

BUZZ: Happens? What happens?

SISSY: You know, people mistakin' me for my sister. My *twin* sister. I heard ol' Feebs was in town here doin' this talk show. Thought I'd drop by, see how she was doin'. It's been a while, ya know.

NICKIE: Oh! We could have done a reunion show!

STAGEHAND: OK. Yeah! The evil twin thing! Of course, it makes sense now! She kills the goody two-shoes sister to gain some sort of big family inheritance and ... then ...

SISSY: Whoa there, buddy! I ain't no evil nuthin' after any family inheritance!

BUZZ: Excuse me, miss, but I'm perplexed.

SISSY: And I'm Sissy Kowalski. Nice to meet ya. But my friends call me Lola. L.O.L.A. Lola.

CANDY: So *you're* Lola. We were led to believe that Phoebe was Lola.

SISSY: That happens all the time as well. Or should I say "happened" all the time.

POLLY: Wait a moment. My sources in Vegas told me that Phoebe had the stage name of Lola. I have documents to prove it. The paychecks she collected were made out to Phoebe St. Self, not Sissy Kowalski.

RICKY: Great. I'm sensing a back story coming on.

SISSY: Right you are Ricky and here it is: Feebs and me never got along. She got everything she wanted. The rich husband, the big house, all the bucks. Me? I got squat! Feebs was a great squat giver. The bigger she got, the more I got squat. You wanna talk about the evil twin, well it was Feebs. She turned the whole family against me. Everyone. I was the designated black sheep.

EDIE: So was I!

CELESTE: *(sadly)* Me too!

NICKIE: Ricky, we should do a whole black sheep show!

SISSY: So, what happened is, I swore I'd get back at Phoebe one day.

NICKIE: Oooh! Tell us more about the "getting back" thing!

SISSY: I hitchhiked around the country for a while, and ended up in Vegas. Got a job in a show as a dancer. Meanwhile, I see that ol' Feebs is makin' quite a name for herself with the home economist racket. So I started thinkin', since we look so much alike, it would be kinda funny if I used that to get even. I used her name for everything. I figured someone like nosy Parker Polly would dig up the dirt and it would all hit the fan.

CANDY: But if you were so bent on revenge, why are you here tonight?

SISSY: Sure, revenge felt great but using Feebs' identity posed a few payroll and tax problems. Plus, I felt a little guilty.

NICKIE: That's OK. Feeling bad is good! Let it out. Can we have some tissues, please?

SISSY: That's just part of it. The other part was the letters.

BUZZ: Letters?

SISSY: Yeah. I was gettin' these weird letters. Some wacko thought he was in love with me.

NICKIE: That's normal. Millions of men write me love letters.

SHECKY: Yeah. Me too.

SISSY: But do they tell you how they like to dress up like Dorothy in the Wizard of Oz?

SHECKY: Some of them, sure.

SISSY: Put butter on your ear lobes and pickled herring between your toes?

SHECKY: A few.

SISSY: I got hundreds of them from the same person! And then they started getting threatening. I thought maybe Phoebe had something to do with it. And this was her way of getting back. Trying to scare me.

NICKIE: Poor thing. What did you do?

SISSY: Well, when the last letter said he was goin' to find me and kill me, so I quit. The next thing you know, I was leavin' Las Vegas.

POLLY: Excuse me for a moment, but the person writing these letters was writing to Phoebe St. Self, correct? Not Sissy Kowalski.

SISSY: Well, that's what I wondered. Phoebe's face was all over the place. Good Housekeeping, Ladies Home Journal, Cigar Aficionado...

EDIE: Sure. The peanut butter lobe loser thought Phoebe was Sissy 'cause when Sissy was Lola, she was being Phoebe, so he thought Lola was Phoebe, but Lola was really Sissy.

SHECKY: *(sarcastic)* Oh yeah. I followed that train of logic!

CANDY: This would explain Phoebe's paranoia. That's why she had checks run on everyone here. That's why she hired me ... or at least my brother. *(to Sissy)* I bet when you quit, the mail got forwarded on to the real Phoebe.

SISSY: Could be. But honey, Phoebe was always paranoid. She used to think my Barbie dolls were giving her disapproving looks.

CANDY: But we can't ignore the fact that she thought someone was out to get her tonight and they did.

STAGEHAND: Yeah! I bet it was the pickled herring dude! He's here tonight!

SHECKY: Well, you can count me out. Herring gives me a rash.

STAGEHAND: There you go, Buzz! It's someone here!

BUZZ: Yes, well ... I think we have enough information to launch a full-scale investigation. I'll just go and, uh ... make a phone call. (*starts to exit*)

ANNOUNCER: Excuse me, people?

SISSY: Who on earth is that?

CELESTE: Yes, Ariel, is that you?

RICKY: No! It's the announcer. Yes, what is it?

ANNOUNCER: I couldn't help but overhear most of what went on this evening, and I think I may be of some assistance.

CANDY: Oh, could you, please? We're awfully tired and we'd all like to go home. We just need some answers.

ANNOUNCER: But, my dear, you've had the answers all along.

CANDY: We have?

ANNOUNCER: Yes. You want to know who wasn't present onstage at the critical moment, right?

CANDY: Well, yes, but we've gone over this. There was Celeste and Polly and the stagehand and me, but ..

ANNOUNCER: Yes, and who else?

CANDY: Who else? (*thinks*) Nobody.

ANNOUNCER: Are you sure?

CELESTE: Ohhhh. I'm getting something.

SHECKY: Yeah, me too. It's called a headache.

CELESTE: Letters. Hundreds of letters. Evil... stalking ... tracking ... Lola ... Phoebe ...

CANDY: I can't think of anyone else.

EDIE: I know! The announcer!

ANNOUNCER: No! Not me! Whose presence is unexplained here tonight? Who just happened to show up here at the show — at the critical moment, well after the murder had taken place?

NICKIE: That one guy out there (*pointing out someone in audience.*)

[As the audience's attention is occupied with the above bit, Buzz makes his way to the area where the announcer sits or stands.]

BUZZ: Ah ha! (*pulls gun*)

[Buzz spins around and points a gun at the cast.]

BUZZ: All right! Nobody move!

NICKIE: (*calmly, still perky*) Oh right. Buzz was also not out here the whole time. And he did happen to show up at the critical moment.

EDIE: But he's a cop!

ANNOUNCER: Are you certain? Did anyone ask to see his badge? Did he show it to anyone?

CANDY: Umm ... well .. not as such.

STAGEHAND: The crazed fan! I was right! Awesome! He's the herring earlobe guy! He could have snuck in and planted the towelettes in her purse when no one was looking.

NICKIE: Right when you were chasing Celeste around!

CELESTE: And then put the crystals on her body to make everyone think it was me!

CANDY: And pretend to be a cop so no one would suspect him! Just like that one Agatha Christie play!

NICKIE: This is great! This is so great!

ANNOUNCER: Excuse me, but this is not so great. I believe he has a gun.

NICKIE: Oh yeah. Not so great.

CANDY: Of course! How could I be so naive! A real cop would have sealed off the area. Forensics would have been brought in to dust for prints. This place would have been swarming with detectives! I did a paper on procedures once. I should have known.

BUZZ: Yeah. You should have known.

SHECKY: Well, you sure fooled us, pal.

BUZZ: No. I was the one who was fooled. I was tricked! I should've known my darling Lola wasn't the woman that was here tonight! It didn't make sense. I didn't know there were two Lolas! But you! (*points gun at Sissy*) You're the real one! The girl I wanted.

SHECKY: Oh, I get it now! That's the one.

BUZZ: Why?! Why didn't you answer my letters?! I loved you! I wanted just one, one little note... a few words ...

SISSY: A few words? Alright. I got two words for you ...

RICKY: Don't do it.

NICKIE: It's a family show, dear. Thanks.

BUZZ: If I couldn't have you, then no one could! You were mine. But then you became this snooty housewife woman! What was up with that? Making crafts and clockwise dishwashing procedures! I want you to dance again. For me! Dance one last time before you die!

SISSY: Yea. I'm not really feeling it right now.

BUZZ: (*threatening with gun*) Dance, I tell you!

SISSY: You're not the boss of me.

RICKY: If I could just interject something at this point. The man does have a gun!

SHECKY: Yeah, babe. I believe dancing would be a good option for you at this juncture.

SISSY: *(To Shecky)* You dance with the guy. He's all nasty and sweaty.

NICKIE: Sweaty? Well, maybe if you wipe your face, sweetie, the nice Lola will dance for you.

[Candy pulls out the unopened towelette and tears top open.]

CANDY: I have just the thing! Here you go, Mr. Buzz.

BUZZ: Huh? Oh, thanks. *(juggles with towelette and gun for a moment)* Here, hold this for me. *(hands gun to Candy, opens towelette and wipes his face)* OK. *(Candy hands gun back to Buzz)* Thanks. All right! Now I'm not sweaty. See? I've wiped it all away with the ... the ... *(dawns on him what he just did)* Oh man! *(falls dead)*

[Polly runs and gets the gun from Buzz, stands over him pointing the gun down at him.]

POLLY: All right, buddy! Don't move! I've got you covered!

RICKY: Uh, Polly? He's, uh ... never mind. Good job.

POLLY: Did they get this on tape? Are they still taping? I can see it now. Polly Pettegolo nabs dangerous killer!

CANDY: I'll go and call the *real* authorities. *(exits)*

CELESTE: *(breaks trance)* I've got it! I've got it! The vision! It came to me! It's Buzz! He's the killer! He's not really a cop! He's ... he's ... *(noticing Buzz on floor)* Oh wow. Far out. Sorry. Little late.

NICKIE: That's OK, Celeste! Isn't that right, Ricky?

RICKY: It sure is, Nickie!

ACT II

NICKIE: Well, Ricky, this has been some show!

RICKY: Yes, it sure has. Of all the shows we've done, this is certainly... one of them.

NICKIE: Who's on tomorrow's show, Ricky?

RICKY: Not real sure, Nickie, but I know *we'll* be there.

NICKIE: That's right! We'll be there, so you be there!

RICKY: Goodnight, everybody!

NICKIE: Bye-bye!

Both wave at camera. Theme music up and out.

ALSO BY LEE MUELLER

Murder Me Always

Death Of A Doornail

An Audition For A Murder

Dead 2 Rights

Remains To Be Seen

An Irritation To A Murder

www.ingramcontent.com/pod-product-compliance
Lightning Source LLC
Chambersburg PA
CBHW032134090426
42743CB00007B/597